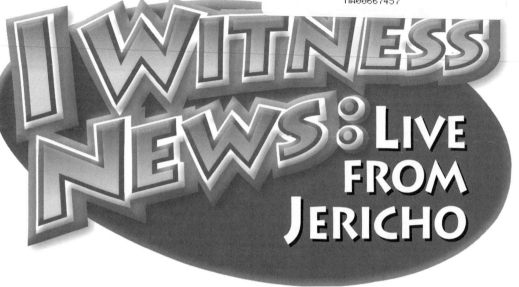

A CHILDREN'S MUSICAL
WITH GOOD NEWS ABOUT GOD'S PROVISION
AND FAITHFULNESS

Created by Peter and Hanneke Jacobs

Singer's Edition

Lillenas PUBLISHING COMPANY

KANSAS CITY, MO 64141

CONTENTS

CHARACTERS

I Witness News Crew

JACK   News Producer (can be played by an adult) - jaded and abrupt, always worried about ratings, dressed in long-sleeved white shirt with rolled up sleeves, with a pencil behind his ear. He has one short singing line, but he can "talk-sing" it if necessary.

CECELIA   Reporter - very vain, should be dressed in suit, always worried about her nails & hair. She may use cue cards for any lines she delivers "on the air." She should have good diction and talk very precisely. She has one short singing line in "We Need A Story."

TERI   Audio Woman - tomboy, dressed in shorts, T-shirt and work boots. She has one short singing line in "We Need A Story."

JOE   Cameraman - the "mature" one. He has been in the business for a long time. He is the only one who can handle Cecelia. Joe may be played by a person with a changed voice. He has one short singing line in "We Need A Story." Dressed in shorts, T-shirt and work boots.

ANNOUNCER   Expressive, clear voice, should have good diction, good microphone technique, and able to project. Also able to time lines to the musical underscores. May be played by any age, and is dressed in modern-day "business" attire. After her/his last line has been delivered (before the song "Giants in the Promised Land") he/she can change and join the choir.

Bible Characters

JOSHUA Leader of the Children of Israel, dressed in Bible costume, carries a walking stick

CALEB Joshua's helper, dressed in Bible costume.

(Note: either Joshua or Caleb should be able to sing the first verse of the song "Be Strong.")

RAHAB Female innkeeper (solo singing voice required "We've All Heard" and "With a Thankful Heart") dressed in fancy Bible costume with gaudy jewelry. If possible, she should be part of the choir when she is not playing the part of Rahab.

SPY 1 and 2 Sent by Joshua to spy out the land of Jericho, dressed in Bible costume.

SOLDIER 1 Male soldier dressed in soldier costume with sword. Soldier 1 does not have a singing part.

SOLDIER 2 Female soldier dressed in soldier costume with sword. Must be a good singer as she sings most of the song, "We Know You're Spies."

4 Choir Members Each have one-liners. Should be able to project without a microphone. Can be combined into 2 parts.

THE PROMISED LAND

WORDS AND MUSIC BY
PETER AND HANNEKE JACOBS
ARRANGED BY PETER JACOBS

With excitement ♩ = ca. 138

all the things of life_____ That make us slip and fall.

We'll keep our eyes_____ look-ing straight a-head_____ And

2nd time to Coda
(to pg. 8, meas. 51)

an-swer to His call._____ I'm

go - in' where the riv - ers are flow - in'. I'm

go - in' where the grapes are grow - in'. I'm

go - in' to the Prom-ised, go - in' to the Prom-ised Land.__

*Narration begins

D.C. al Coda
(to pg. 6, meas. 1)

*NARRATOR #1: Be strong and of good courage. Do not be afraid, nor be dismayed for the Lord your God is with you wherever you go. *(Joshua 1:9)*

NARRATOR #2: Every place that the sole of your foot will tread upon, I have given to you. *(Joshua 1:3)*

ANNOUNCER: The following program uses Time-Delay Satellite technology, designed so that you could witness history. *(rapidly)* No animals were harmed during the making of this program. This program is not recommended for viewers who lack imagination. God's Word is never void even where prohibited. Actual price has been paid in full. Please refer to God's Word for complete details.

(music begins) (Underscore No. 1)

ANNOUNCER: This is an I Witness News special report. And now, here is your I Witness News reporter, Cecelia Barnhurst. Cecelia?

(Cecelia, Joe & Teri are somewhere in one of the aisles. Cecelia has a hand-held microphone in her hand. She is speaking to a camera held by Joe. Teri listens intently to whatever is being said into her headphones. Jack is standing onstage scowling, with his hands on his waist.)

CECELIA: Good afternoon. I'm standing in front of...Bobo the Chimp, in his brand new cage. For awhile it seemed that Bobo was not too happy about it...I'm told that before we arrived he was screaming and banging his head against the bars. But since he found that little mirror in the corner of his cage, he seems to be quite content to look at his reflection.

JACK: *(muttering to himself)* Now THERE'S something Cecelia should be able to relate to!

CECELIA: *(with a dirty look to Jack)* That must be STATIC I hear from either Bobo OR my producer. I can't tell the difference. *(with fake smile to the camera)* Reporting from the zoo, this is Cecelia Barnhurst, with I Witness News, wishing you a wonderful day. *(fake smile)*

TERI: *(pause)* And...we're clear. Good work, everyone.

(Cecelia holds her smile until the camera goes off, then immediately begins to scowl. Teri removes her headphones and hands them to Joe. News Crew immediately walks on-stage into the newsroom and sits down. Cecelia begins to file her nails. Jack paces back and forth in front of them.)

CECELIA: I heard that last comment, Jack! And for your information, I can't stand these zoo stories anymore! *(turning to Jack, pouting)* When am I going to get a REAL story?

(Jack lifts his hands up in dismissal.)

JACK: Cece, We've been over this a million times! People like baby animals, so we give them baby animals...

CECELIA: Jack, this is NOT news! My contract says I'm supposed to report the NEWS, not some fluff zoo piece every day! *(she whines)* Everybody else gets to use the Time-Delay Satellite! When do I get to use it?

(Cecelia throws her notes down on the floor in a display of temper and looks at her hand in dismay.)

CECELIA: Oooohh! Now you made me break a nail! *(sucks her injured finger as Joe and Teri shake their heads.)*

JACK: *(growling at her)* See, this is exactly what I mean! You want to report real news, but you're too worried about your hair and your nails! Aw, tell her, Joe!

CECELIA: *(pleading to Joe instead)* Joe, YOU know what I want! You've been doing this all your life! *(she stamps her foot)* I want a NEWS story!

JOE: *(putting his hand on her shoulder)* Now, Cece, calm down. You'll get your chance.

JACK: *(disgustedly)* She HAD her chance and she blew it! Who else but Cecelia Barnhurst could be late to the parting of the Red Sea because she was having a bad hair day? *(throws up his hands in disgust)* You know, it's a good thing the other network's helicopter rescued you or you'd be down at the bottom with the whole Egyptian army!

CECELIA: Jack, you know I couldn't go on the air looking like THAT!

JACK: *(scarcastically)* And so, instead, you miss the miracle of the millenium! Look, I'm tired of the other networks scooping us on every news story! Today we got beaten in the ratings by a re-run of "Pharoah Knows Best!"

JOE: You know, Jack, what we need is an exclusive. Something the other networks don't have.

(music begins)

WE NEED A STORY

WORDS AND MUSIC BY
PETER AND HANNEKE JACOBS
ARRANGED BY PETER JACOBS

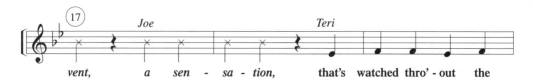

need!

JACK: Okay everybody. Let's put our heads together
and see if we can come up with something great!

Teri

May - be   we   could   find   a   high - speed

chase.   *Ev - 'ry - bo - dy   loves*   a

high - speed   chase!   With   chop - pers   in   the

rit.   *a tempo*

air,   lights and   si - rens ev - 'ry - where.   It's got

ev - 'ry - thing that   peo - ple want to   see.   Yes,

that's   the   kind   of   sto - ry   that   we   need!

JACK: Hey, great idea! Now all we have to do is
stake-out about a thousand roads! C'mon, you
people! Give me a story I can do something with!

News crew and Choir

What we real - ly need is a sto - ry,

A "turn on the news" kind of

sto - ry. An e - vent, a sen -

sa - tion, that's watched thro' - out the na - tion. Our

rat - ings would soar, yes in - deed. If we

just had the sto - ry that we need!

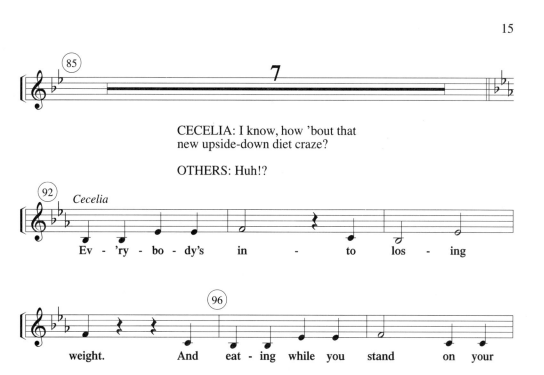

CECELIA: I know, how 'bout that
new upside-down diet craze?

OTHERS: Huh!?

Ev - 'ry - bo - dy's   in   to   los -   ing

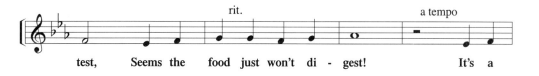

weight.   And   eat - ing   while   you   stand   on   your

head   *is*   *great!*   They've   put   it   to   the

test,   Seems the   food   just won't di - gest!   It's a

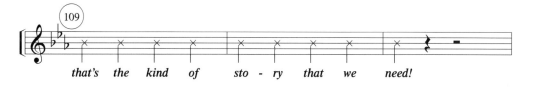

mir - a - cle   for   di - et   his - to - ry.   Yes,

that's   the   kind   of   sto - ry   that   we   need!

15

JACK *(more exasperated)*: Ah, that's just dandy! First she complains about doing a zoo story, the next minute, she wants to cover some crazy diet fad! Where on earth did I find you people? Somebody get me an aspirin!

News crew and Choir

What we real - ly need is a sto - ry,

A "turn on the news" kind of

sto - ry. An e - vent, a sen -

sa - tion, that's watched thro' - out the na - tion. Our

rat - ings would soar, yes in - deed. If we

just had the sto - ry that we need!

14

JOE: Hey everybody, do you remember that story
we did a few years ago about Moses leading those
Hebrews out of slavery in Egypt?

OTHERS: Yeah?

JOE: Well listen to this. They're headed this way!

The peo - ple of God are al - most here. They've wan - dered thro' the des - ert for for - ty years. *God prom - ised them a land* That is in an - oth - er's hand. This could be an - oth - er mir - a - cle to see. Yes, that's the kind of sto - ry that we

18

poco rit., swing
Jack

182 *News crew* a tempo, straight

need! I real - ly like it! That's the kind of

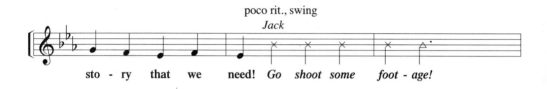

poco rit., swing
Jack

sto - ry that we need! *Go shoot some foot - age!*

186 a tempo, straight
News crew and Choir

Divisi

That's the kind of sto - ry that we

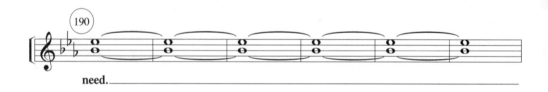

190

need.

5

JACK: Well what are you all standing
around for? Go get me that story!

201

2

(As the song ends, Cecelia, Joe and Teri quickly grab their gear and run into the "Wilderness Base Camp" area in front of the choir.)

(Wilderness base camp: Joe and Teri begin to set-up their "equipment" getting ready to go on the air. Teri puts on her headphones, Joe picks up the video camera. Cecelia is fussing with her makeup.)

CECELIA: This is SO great. A REAL story at last. *(rummaging in her purse)* Oh, where did I put my cactus flower lipstick?

TERI: *(motioning to Cecilia)* Ten seconds to air, Cece!

CECELIA: *(getting frusterated)* Oh, the things I put up with!

(Cecelia is frantically trying to put lipstick on with one hand, holding a hand mirror in the other hand.)

TERI: Seven seconds!

CECELIA: Oh, here it is!

TERI: In 5, 4, 3, 2...

CECELIA: *(as Teri counts down)* Can't you see I'm not ready yet, Teri...?!!! *(with a loud sigh)* Aargh!

(music begins) (Underscore No. 2)

ANNOUNCER: Our regularly scheduled program, "Cooking with Manna" will not be seen at this time, so that we may bring you the following I Witness News Special Report.

ANNOUNCER: *(waits a few beats to let the new theme music be established)* We take you now LIVE, via Time-Delay Satellite, to Cecelia Barnhurst, with this fast-breaking news story! Cecelia?

(Cecelia quickly puts down the lipstick and mirror, picks up the microphone and addresses the video camera with a plastic smile. Joshua is standing next to her.)

CECELIA: I'm standing in the midst of the Israeli camp, just east of the Jordan River. For those of you who have not been following this story, these people have been literally wandering around in circles for the past 40 years since their miraculous escape from the Pharaoh and his armies. They're headed for what they believe to be their Promised Land. I'm joined now by Joshua, the leader of the Israelites. Tell me, Joshua, how do you intend on taking this land?

JOSHUA: Well, I'm going to ask for a couple of volunteers to go behind the enemy lines and spy out the situation.

CECELIA: I understand that you were one of the original spies who did this exact same thing forty years ago, and that's when the trouble all began.

JOSHUA: Well, the last time we went into this land, there were twelve of us. And with the exception of my good friend, Caleb, everyone got pretty scared when they saw how big those people really were!

CECELIA: Really? How big were they?

JOSHUA: Well, let us tell you about it...

(Joe and Teri continue to "film" during the song. Joshua steps back in front of the choir, Cecelia moves back out of the action.)

(music begins)

GIANTS IN THE PROMISED LAND

WORDS AND MUSIC BY
PETER AND HANNEKE JACOBS
ARRANGED BY PETER JACOBS

Sneaky ♩ = ca. 112

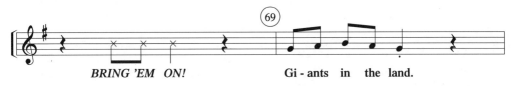

BRING 'EM ON!   Gi - ants in the land.

WHO CARES?!   'Bout the gi - ants in the

Prom - ised Land.

(After song, the News Crew and Joshua move back to their former "interview" positions. Caleb walks past, and Cecelia calls out to him. The Two Spies should be ready to come forward in a bit.)

CECELIA: Oh, there's Caleb now! *(she calls out)* Excuse me, Mr. Caleb, yoo hoo! Could you join us in this interview?

CALEB: Yes ma'am. *(he waves at the camera)* Hi mom!

(Caleb joins Joshua on camera. Joshua pokes Caleb to get him back on track.)

CECELIA: Well, Mr. Caleb, Do you also believe that things will be different this time?

CALEB: Well, our people have learned an important lesson since the last time we went over there. God had to keep us wandering in the wilderness for 40 years...until we learned to really trust Him.

CECELIA: *(missing the point)* Forty years? In the wilderness? Let me make sure I understand this...You had NO running water? NO showers? No manicures? Ughhh! *(she shivers)*

CALEB: Yes, well, most of the older people are no longer with us. But their children are grown up now, and have seen many miracles. Our faith and our courage are stronger now.

JOSHUA: You see, Caleb and I have always believed that God was bigger than any problems we might face. And now our people believe it too. Now, if you'll excuse us, we need to go get some volunteers.

(The two spies quickly come forward.)

CALEB: I've already gotten them, Joshua.

SPY 1: We're ready to go!

SPY 2: Just say the word.

JOSHUA: *(to the spies)* You should leave now so you can get into Jericho before the city gates close for the night.

(The spies start down the center aisle towards the back.)

CALEB: *(lifting up his hand in blessing)* Go in the name of the Lord!

(Cecelia runs after the two spies trying to get an interview with them. Joe and Teri have to scramble to keep her "on camera".)

CECELIA: *(a little out of breath)* Uh, excuse me, spies? Could I get a quick word with you for the viewers at home?

SPY 1: Sorry ma'am!

SPY 2: No comment!

(Spies exit out the back. Joe and Teri keep the camera on Cecelia as she comes back. Cecelia addresses the camera.)

CECELIA: *(sigh)* This is Cecelia Barnhurst reporting live from the Jordan River.

TERI: *(pause)* And...we're clear. Great job everybody.

(News Crew begins to pack up their equipment.)

CECELIA: *(wiping her forehead)* Ohhhh...this desert climate really dries out my face! I need a mud bath. *(goes up to someone in the choir)* Uh... Excuse me, can you direct me to the nearest day spa? I hear they have really great day spas out here in the desert!

(Cecelia takes the microphone and holds it out to one of the choir members to answer. Choir member shakes his/her head.)

CHOIR MEMBER 1: Uh, sorry. I don't know of any...*(shrugs shoulders)*

CECELIA: *(lamenting)* No day spa? *(overly dramatic)* Oh, Joe! There's no day spa out here! What am I gonna dooooo!?

JOE: Forget about a day spa, Cece! You wanted a news story and you've got one! Come on, let's follow those spies.

(News Crew quickly grabs their equipment and runs after the spies down the center aisle and out the back. Josuha lifts his stick, and addresses the choir.)

JOSHUA: People of Israel. Be strong! Be courageous! *(music begins)* You are the chosen people of God, so don't be afraid! God has promised us this land! And what God has promised, He delivers!

Be Strong

WORDS AND MUSIC BY
PETER AND HANNEKE JACOBS
ARRANGED BY PETER JACOBS

PLEASE NOTE: Copying of this product is not covered by CCLI licenses. For CCLI information call 1-800-234-2446.

(The following dialogue takes place in the audience as Cecelia, Joe and Teri are wandering through Jericho, an aisle in the audience, following the spies. Teri and Joe are loaded down with gear. Cecelia is carrying only her makeup bag, and is in thoroughly bad mood.)

(music begins) (Underscore No. 3)

(News Crew enters through the audience arguing all the way.)

CECELIA: *(to Joe and Teri)* I can't believe you let those spies get away! You guys were supposed to be watching them!

TERI: *(sighing)* We were right behind them...until YOU had to stop at the store!

CECELIA: Well, excuuuuse me! I was running low on make-up. What did you expect me to do, Teri? I can't go on the air looking like I just stepped out of the shower!

TERI: *(scarcastically)* Oh, no, we couldn't have that! Well at least we've found a motel so we can spend the night.

(As the News Crew comes onto the stage, the lights come up on Rahab's Inn where Rahab and the two spies are sitting down in the chairs talking. When the News Crew arrives, Rahab gets up and goes behind the counter to check them in. The News Crew doesn't notice the two spies.)

RAHAB: Good evening. My name is Rahab. May I help you?

JOE: Yes ma'am, we'd like three rooms, please.

CECELIA: *(being rather pushy)* And MY room needs to have a jacuzzi tub, AND I'll need extra towels, AND I don't want to be next to the ice machine, OR the elevator, AND...I don't want...

RAHAB: *(politely interrupting)* I'm sorry, ma'am, but we only have two rooms left.

JOE: I'm sure they'll be fine. We'll take them.

CECELIA: *(through clenched teeth)* Joe!

JOE: The Jericho gates are closed for the night, Cece! Where else are we gonna go? You're just going to have to share with Teri!

CECELIA: *(dramatically)* Oh, I need a shower, then room service. *(She gives a caustic look at Rahab.)* Pleeeaaase tell me you have room service?!

(Rahab shakes her head no.)

CECELIA: *(sigh)* You don't. What kind of place is this with NO ROOM SERVICE?

(Rahab takes some money from Joe and hands him two keys.)

RAHAB: *(pointing to the "To Rooms" sign)* That'll be rooms 413 and 415. Just walk through this hall and take the elevator to the 4th floor. *(trying not to laugh)* The rooms are located right next to the ice machine.

CECELIA: *(complaining very loudly)* THE ICE MACHINE!???

(Joe and Teri drag her offstage as Cecelia continues complaining loudly.)

CECELIA: *(continues ad-lib)* Joe! I told you, I need a jacuzzi-tub, and...they don't even have room service, and I can NOT room with Teri, she probably snores...THIS IS NOT IN MY CONTRACT!

(Rahab changes the sign from "Vacancy" to "No Vacancy", appears to lock the front door, and turns her attention back to the two spies.)

RAHAB: Looks like we're completely full for the night now. Listen, as I was saying, I know the two of you are spies from Israel, and I know why you're here. We've all heard about this God of yours.

SPY 2: Tell us. What have you heard?

(music begins)

RAHAB: Well...everybody has been talking about how great and powerful this God of yours is...and how no one is able to stand in His way.

We've All Heard

WORDS AND MUSIC BY
PETER AND HANNEKE JACOBS
ARRANGED BY PETER JACOBS

might - y hand. And we've all heard

of all____ He's done. The Lord____ is

great____ and might - y, He has awe - some

pow - er and we know____ His bat - tle will____ be won.

Divisi

Well, we've all heard.

Rahab (2nd time)

We've all heard,_____

Yes, we've all heard. We've

might - y, He has awe - some pow - er. He is great___ and might - y, He has awe - some pow - er. And we know His bat - tle___ will___ be won.

RAHAB: Okay, listen. Our king knows that you two are here somewhere, and he has soldiers looking all over the city for you. So I'll make a deal with you. I will hide you from them and I'll help you escape if you promise to spare my family and me when your people take this city.

SPY 2: *(shaking her hand in agreement)* All right. We will see that no harm comes to you or your family.

SPY 1: Just make sure that you stay inside this inn or we won't be able to guarantee your safety.

(The two soldiers begin banging on the door. If the door is not visible on your stage, than you should hear the sound of banging on the door from offstage.)

RAHAB: *(in a stage whisper)* Soldiers!

SOLDIER 1: *(from off-stage)* Open up in there.

RAHAB: *(loudly)* I'm sorry, we're full for the night.

SOLDIER 2: Open up in the name of the king!

RAHAB: *(stage whisper to the spies)* Quick, you must hide. If they find you, they will kill you. I'll try to stall them.

(The spies duck behind the check-in counter, out of view of the soldiers. Rahab opens the door and two soldiers brandishing swords almost mow her down as they enter.)

SOLDIER 1: We're looking for two men. They're about yeah-tall and they're wanted by the king for spying!

SOLDIER 2: We heard they came in here!

RAHAB: *(thinking fast)* Yes...well...uh...they were here...but...uh, they left. We were out of rooms for the night. They went that way. *(she points back the way they came)* I'm sure you can still catch them if you hurry.

SOLDIER 1: Not so fast! We've got orders to search this place from top to bottom! Stand aside!

SOLDIER 2: Let's check the hallway.

(Soldiers exit off stage in same direction as News Crew exited. As soon as they're gone, the spies come out from behind the check-in counter.)

SPY 1: *(looking over his shoulder)* Wow! I thought they'd find us for sure!

RAHAB: You can't stay here. It's too dangerous. We have to get you both out of the city tonight. Listen, I can lower you over the city wall from this window. Just don't forget what you promised me!

SPY 1: You have our word. No harm will come to you, or your family as long as you all remain inside of this house.

RAHAB: Now quickly. You must go. If you can make it to the Jordan River, you'll be safe.

(Rahab takes rope hanging over the window and two spies climb through the window opening, and disappear from view. Soldiers enter from the hallway with the News Crew as prisoners.)

SOLDIER 2: *(scarcastically)* Well, look what we have here! They look like spies to me. Don't you think?

SOLDIER 1: Yeah, look at this one *(points to Cecelia)*. You aren't from around here, are ya, Missy?

CECELIA: *(arrogantly)* Oh, pleeease! We are NOT spies! We're just news reporters.

SOLDIER 2: You came in just before the city walls closed! You snuck into this inn, and these bags you're carrying probably contain goods stolen from our people! You're spies, and that's all there is to it!

(music begins)

WE KNOW YOU'RE SPIES

WORDS AND MUSIC BY
PETER AND HANNEKE JACOBS
ARRANGED BY PETER JACOBS

You will soon re - al - ize, de - cep - tion is not ver - y

wise. We know you're spies!

2. You

Solo

Now you've bro - ken all the rules. Do

Choir

you take us all for fools? We know you're spies!

So don't make up lies! You will

soon re - al - ize, de - cep - tion is not ver - y wise.

We know you're spies!

CECELIA: You have got to be kidding me. I'm not a spy! Get your hands off me!

We know you're spies!

CECELIA: Come on. If I break a nail, you are in big trouble, Mister!

We know you're spies!

(During the short instrumental portion after the second chorus of the song, the soldiers are busy tying up the News Crew, looking into their bags and inspecting the camera equipment, obviously not knowing what it is. Rahab nervously looks out the window from time to time.)

SOLDIER 2: Yep! They're spies all right! And these gadgets prove it! *(holds up a video camera)*

TERI: Those so-called gadgets are expensive cameras! State of the art, I might add!

SOLDIER 1: A likely story! Take them to the king!

CECELIA: *(to the soldiers)* Hey! Get your hands off me!

SOLDIER 2: Sorry, Missy! You're coming with us! The king wants to speak with you!

CECELIA: *(arrogantly)* You obviously don't know who you're dealing with, here, Buster! Hey! Watch where you point that spear! Look, we're just reporters, okay? We don't MAKE the news here, we just REPORT it! Hello??!!!! Teri? Joe? Wanna help me out here?

SOLDIER 1: Look, lady, I don't care if you're Barbara Walters! We have orders! Take them away!

(Soldiers march the News Crew offstage, Cecelia struggling and protesting all the way.)

CECELIA: Wait! At least let me take my makeup bag! Stop that! You'll break one of my nails! You guys are gonna hear from my lawyer!!!!

(music begins) (Underscore No. 4)

(Soldiers exit with News Crew)

(The scene shifts back to the Wilderness Base Camp, in front of the choir risers. The spies enter through an aisle in the audience. Joshua and several kids from the choir come forward to greet them as they approach the stage. Spies do not speak until they reach the stage.)

SPY 2: That was close!

SPY 1: You got that right! Thank God we made it out of Jericho and back to the Jordan River.

SPY 2: Look! There's Joshua!

JOSHUA: *(meeting them)* Greetings! Tell me! What did you find out in Jericho?

SPY 1: The entire city is afraid of us because of the power of our God!

JOSHUA: *(to the choir)* Praise be to God! Word of all His great miracles has even reached the Promised Land!

(Choir cheers)

JOSHUA: The time has come for us to cross the Jordan River and enter into the Promised Land! This is the time our fathers waited and prayed for, and God has chosen to deliver this land into OUR hands! Stand back!

(Music begins. Choir gasps, oohs and ahs as everyone looks down the center aisle.)

CHOIR MEMBER 2: Look! The waters are parting!

CHOIR MEMBER 3: It's just like what happened at the Red Sea!

CHOIR MEMBER 4: It's a miracle!

JOSHUA: And as we enter this land God is giving us, let us stop to thank Him, for God has given us another miracle!

GLORIFY GOD WITH MY PRAISE

WORDS AND MUSIC BY
PETER AND HANNEKE JACOBS
ARRANGED BY PETER JACOBS

_____ to the Lord, all the earth._____ Yes, give

glo - ry and hon - or and praise_____ to the Lord, all the earth._

_____ I bow down be - fore_____ You here in

this ho - ly place._____ Now and for - ev - er, Lord_____

I'll seek Your face_____ and I'll sing of Your good - ness and

(to pg. 44, meas. 10)
Choir

glo - ri - fy God_ with my_____ praise._____ For_

Solo

_ praise._____ And I'll sing of Your good - ness and

rit.

glo - ri - fy God_____ with my_____ praise._____

JOSHUA: Praise be to the Lord our God!

CROWD: *(in unison)* Praise be to the Lord our God!

(Lights go off the choir and the action shifts to the news room.)

(music begins) (Underscore No. 5)

(Jack's cell phone rings at the end of the underscore.)

JACK: *(answering his cell phone)* Hello? Yes, this is Jack. Who's this? *(pause)* The Jericho sheriff's office? Oh, good! Look, the people you are holding are NOT spies! They are a news crew! *(pause)* What's a news crew? It's a team of people who...oh, never mind! Look, they are NOT your spies! *(pause)* Yeah, yeah, yeah, okay, I promise...it'll never happen again! Fine...just let them go now, okay? Great. Thank you. Can you put 'em on the phone?

(Jack begins to pace back and forth.)

JACK: *(talking to himself)* Unbelievable! The greatest miracle of our time, and where is my News Crew? In a jail cell in Jericho! Unbelievable! *(pause)* Hello? Joe? Yeah, yeah...look, I had to call in a few favors to get you released. *(pause)* No, I don't wanna hear about it. Just get back on the story. I don't want to get scooped by another network again!

(Jack slams his phone shut or hangs up if it's a desk-phone.)

JACK: Unbelievable!

(music begins)

(Lights go back up on the choir as Joshua addresses them. He is walking back and forth in front of the choir with his walking-stick.)

JOSHUA: Chosen people of God, the time has come. God is giving us the city of Jericho. Each day, He has commanded us to walk around the city one time. Then on the seventh day, we will walk around the city seven times. And finally, when the trumpets give one long, loud blast, everyone needs to shout as loud as you can! THEN you will all see the mighty power of God!!

CALEB: Remember what God told us back in the wilderness? "Be strong and be of good courage; for the Lord our God is with us wherever we go!"

Our God Will Never Fail

WORDS AND MUSIC BY
PETER AND HANNEKE JACOBS
ARRANGED BY PETER JACOBS

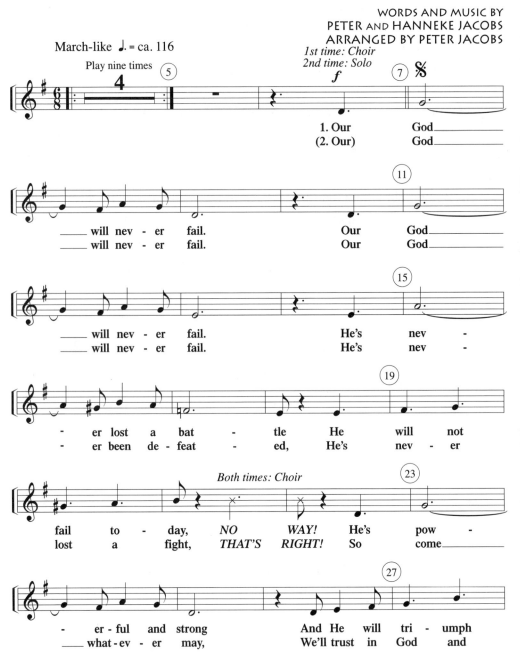

50

So in God we stand, the Vic - to - ry's at

hand, 'Cause He will nev - er fail._____

(After the song ends, the News Crew enters from backstage.)

CECELIA: *(rubbing her neck)* Aughh! What a night! I need a back massage! Let's get out of here!

JOE: *(pointing to those walking around the audience)* Wait! Look at all the people walking around the city!

CECELIA: *(unconcerned)* People are walking around the city...so?

JOE: Don't you see? There's going to be another miracle! Come on, Teri, we'll set up right here...

(Teri and Joe begin setting up their equipment.)

CECELIA: *(stamping her foot furiously)* Joe! I'm sweaty, hot, tired and I need my nails done! I can't go on the air looking like this!

JOE: Look, Cece, there are no other networks here. Something is going to happen, I can feel it! Do you want to do real news or not?

CECELIA: There IS no news, Joe! *(she starts to whine)* I just wanna sit in a nice warm tub...is that too much to ask? I wanna go home!!!

JOE: Wait! Look at that!

CECELIA: Look at what? They walk, they go home. They walk, they go home. They walk SEVEN TIMES today, and they STOP. That's NOT NEWS! Let's go.

(Joe and Teri continue setting up their equipment. Cecilia puts her hands on her waist in defiance.)

JOE: *(putting his foot down)* We're staying here! If you don't do the newscast, I will!

CECELIA: *(disgustedly)* Oh, pleeease, Joe! You look worse than I do! *(sighing)* All right, I'll do it, but then I'm going home!

(Cecelia takes the microphone, puts on a plastic smile, and addresses the camera. News Crew stays onstage. Joshua goes down to lead the group of small children. While Cecelia talks, the camera is on her.

(music begins)

CECELIA: Good afternoon. This is Cecelia Barnhurst with late breaking news, just outside the city of Jericho. The people of Israel have walked around this city for the past 6 days without saying a single word. Today is the seventh day and they have now walked around this city 7 times.

(During the song, Joe appears to be filming the children walking around the audience. After the second verse. Joshua raises his stick. Several of the little children raise horns and appear to blow them as Cecelia describes the action.)

JOSHUA FOUGHT THE BATTLE OF JERICHO

TRADITIONAL
ARRANGED BY PETER JACOBS

Jer - i - cho____ and the walls came a - tum - bl - in' down! Up

to the walls____ of Jer - i - cho____ he marched with spear in hand.__

____ "Now blow those trum - pets", Josh - u - a cried,__ "'Cause the

bat - tle is in God's hands."____ O Josh-ua fought the bat-tle of

Jer - i - cho,____ Jer - i - cho,____ Jer - i - cho.____

Josh - ua fought the bat - tle of Jer - i - cho____ and the

walls came a - tum - bl - in' down!

CECELIA: Wait a minute! Everyone has stopped. I'm looking over at Joshua…He's shouting something to the people. Wait! Wait, Joe, get a close-up of that! Several people are holding what looks to me like ram's horns, and now they're blowing those horns like trumpets!

CECELIA: All of a sudden this crowd is shouting. I'm not sure what this is all about. Wait a second…O my word! I can hardly believe my eyes, but it seems…yes, the walls surrounding the city of Jericho have fallen down.

Jer - i - cho,_____ Jer - i - cho,_____ Jer - i - cho._____

Josh - ua fought the bat - tle of Jer - i - cho_____ and the

walls came a - tum-bl - in' down! and the walls came a - tum-bl - in'

Divisi

down! And the walls came tum -

blin' down!_____

and the walls came a-tum-bl - in' down!

(When song is over, the choir cheers. The children who were walking around the audience sit down on the floor in front. An adult quickly collects the flags.)

CECELIA: *(into the mike)* I can't believe what we've just seen! This huge wall surrounding Jericho has just fallen down and collapsed in front of our very eyes! No explosives were used; just the sound of horns blowing and people shouting! This is news in the making, brought to you EXCLUSIVELY by your I Witness News team! Today we have witnessed a miracle! *(mouth wide open in astonishment)* This is Cecelia Barnhurst reporting live from Jericho.

SOUND EFFECT CUE: CELL PHONE RINGS

(Joe answers his phone. It's Jack on the other end, but we don't see or hear him.)

JOE: Hello? Hi Jack! Did you see that! Wasn't that the most amazing thing you've ever seen! *(he listens)* The phones? They're going crazy at the station? Cool! Thanks, man! Wait, here comes Joshua. I gotta go! I've got to shake this man's hand! Teri, take the camera for a second.

(He hangs up the phone as Joshua comes over to be interviewed. Teri takes over the camera.)

JOE: *(shaking his hand)* Joshua, I am honored to meet you! For myself, and also for our viewers who are watching right now, can you tell me how these walls just fell down...by themselves?

CECELIA: Hey! That's MY interview, Joe!

JOE: *(shushing her)* Calm down, Cece! You'll get the next interview! So, Joshua, just how did those walls fall down?

JOSHUA: This was an act of God, not something that happened by itself! We have been on a journey for 40 years, and God has done many miracles in that time. But only those who were strong and courageous were able to make it to the Promised Land.

JOE: So...those who had faith in God were rewarded?

JOSHUA: That is exactly what happened. It is God who has done all the miracles that we have seen and to Him we give all the glory!

(Joe goes back to the camera and Cecelia interviews Rahab.)

TERI: Okay, Cece, your turn. Go interview Rahab.

CECELIA: *(with a dirty look at Joe & Teri)* Aww...why do I always get stuck with the girl? *(she waves at Rahab)* Miss Rahab! Yoo-hoo! *(fake smile)* How nice to see you again!

RAHAB: Yes, well, I'm glad to see all of you made it safely out of Jericho before the walls fell!

CECELIA: Well, Rahab, congratulations! You and your family are the only survivors of the city of Jericho! What are you going to do now?

RAHAB: *(she breaks character for a moment and is very excited)* I'm going to Dis...*(she catches herself and becomes more serious)* I mean, I'm going to do some quiet reflecting.

CECELIA: Really?

RAHAB: Well, frankly, I am still in awe of the power of the God of Israel! *(music begins)* I'm so thankful that He chose to spare me and my family, out of this entire city of Jericho. I want to make the God of Israel my God from now on! He is mighty and powerful! *(she gets on her knees, looks up and lifts her hands up to the Lord)* May the God of Israel be praised now and forevermore!

With a Thankful Heart

WORDS AND MUSIC BY
PETER AND HANNEKE JACOBS
ARRANGED BY PETER JACOBS

thank - ful heart, Fa - ther, I will

sing.

(to pg. 59, meas. 19)

sing. With a

thank - ful heart I will sing Your

praise. For Your faith - ful -

ness in so man - y ways.

For the mer - cy You have shown me,

For the love You bring.

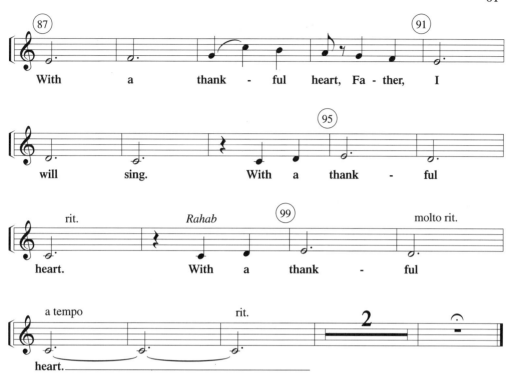

87 With a thank - ful heart, Fa - ther, I **91**

will sing. **95** With a thank - ful

rit. *Rahab* **99** molto rit.

heart. With a thank - ful

a tempo rit. **2**

heart.

JOSHUA: *(putting his hand on Rahab's shoulder)* Rahab, God has honored your courage and from now on you are welcome among us.

RAHAB: Thank you, Joshua. I will spend the rest of my life serving God! *(slight laugh)* I guess I'll have to find a new job, too.

JOSHUA: *(addressing both the choir and the audience)* Let us always remember what God has done today. And no matter what the future holds, we can have courage, for God is always with us!

(music begins)

CECELIA: *(looking into the camera)* Well, there you have it! This is Cecelia Barnhurst for I Witness News, signing off from Jericho via Time-Delay Satellite. Thank you all for joining us, and good night!

THE PROMISED LAND
REPRISE

WORDS AND MUSIC BY
PETER AND HANNEKE JACOBS
ARRANGED BY PETER JACOBS